Insects

Revised and updated

Rod Theodorou

Heinemann Library
Chicago, Illinois

Customer Service 888-454-2279
Visit our website at www.heinemannraintree.com

Designed by Joanna Hinton-Malivoire
Printed and bound in China by South China Printing Co. Ltd.

11 10 09 08 07
10 9 8 7 6 5 4 3 2 1
10-digit ISBN 1-40349-244-1 (hb)   10-digit ISBN 1-40349-251-4 (pb)
13-digit ISBN 978-1-4034-9244-9 (hb)   13-digit ISBN 978-1-4034-9251-7 (pb)

The Library of Congress has cataloged the first edition of this book as follows:

Theodorou, Rod.
    Insects / Rod Theodorou.
        p.   cm. — (Animal babies)
    Includes bibliographical references (p.   ) and index.
    Summary: Introduces the birth, development, care, feeding, and
characteristics of insect young.
    ISBN 1-57572-880-X (lib. bdg.)
    1. Insects—Infancy—Juvenile literature. 2. Parental behavior in
animals—Juvenile literature. [1. Insects. 2. Animal—Infancy.
3. Parental behavior in animals.] I. Title. II. Series: Animal
babies (Des Plaines, Ill.)
QL495.5.T48 1999
595.713'9—dc21   99-18052
                                               CIP

Acknowledgements
The publishers would like to thank the following for permission to reproduce photographs:
Ardea: Ken Lucas p. 30; BBC: Hans Christoph Kappel
p. **6**, Pete Oxford p. **9**; Creatas p. **4** bottom left; Digital Stock p. **4** top right and middle left; Digital Vision
p. **4** bottom right; Frank Lane: B Borrell p. **13**; Nature P L: Wegner/ARCO p. **8**; Getty Images / Photodisc
p. **4** top left and middle right; NHPA: Martin Harvey p. **7**, Anthony Bannister p. **22**, Stephen Dalton pp. **17**, **18**, **24**;
Oxford Scientific Films: Phil Devries p. **5**, Tim Shepherd p. **10**, Scott Camazine p. **11**, Avril Ramage
p. **12**, J H Robinson, p. **15**, K G Vock p. **16**, G I Bernard p. **19**, P & W Ward pp. **20**, **21**, Neil Bromhall, p. **23**; Tony
Stone: Art Wolfe p. **14**.
Cover photograph of a silk moth caterpillar reproduced with permission of Corbis/Volkmar Brockhaus;Zefa.

Every effort has been made to contact copyright holders of any material reproduced in this book. Any omissions will be rectified in subsequent printings if notice is given to the publishers.

The paper used to print this book comes from sustainable resources.

Contents

Some words are shown in bold, **like this**. You can find out what they mean by looking in the Glossary.

Introduction

There are many different types of animals. All animals have babies. They care for their babies in different ways.

These are the six main animal groups.

Mammal

 Bird

Amphibian

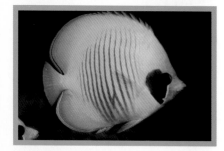 Fish

Reptile

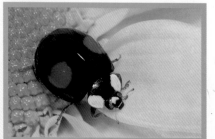 Insect

beetle young

adult beetle

This is an adult fungus beetle next to its young.

This book is about insects. There are more insects in the world than any other kind of animal. Most lay eggs. The young often look very different than their parents.

What Is an Insect?

All adult insects:

- have three parts to their bodies
- have six legs
- have two feelers called antennae.

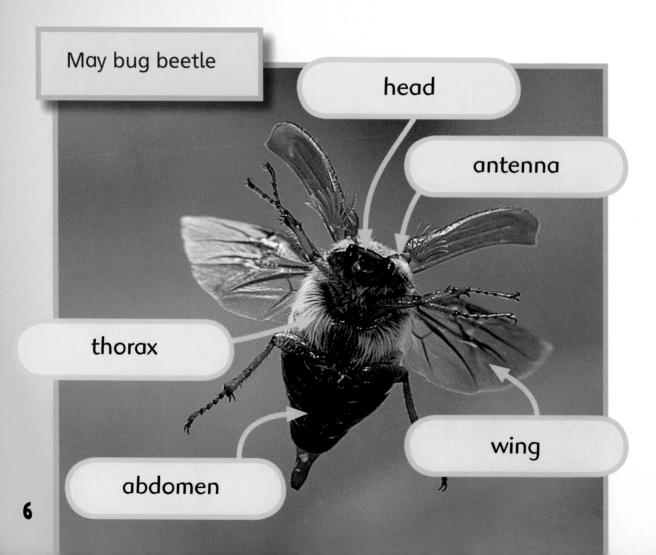

May bug beetle

head

antenna

thorax

wing

abdomen

6

When this giant atlas silk moth is at rest it leaves its four wings open.

Most insects:

- have two or four wings to help them fly
- lay eggs that **hatch** into babies.

Laying Eggs

This butterfly is laying its eggs on a leaf.

egg

Most insects lay their eggs near a plant or a dead animal. When their young **hatch** they will have something to eat.

Some wasps sting a caterpillar or beetle and put it into a hole. They lay an egg in this hole, so the young will have something to eat when it hatches.

sand wasp

caterpillar

This sand wasp is dragging a caterpillar to its **burrow** for its young to eat.

Caring for the Eggs

Most insects do not take care of their eggs. Once they have laid them they just fly away. A few insects do stay with their eggs and young. They keep them safe from **enemies**.

This female earwig looks after her eggs.

eggs

egg cell

Worker bees take care of the **queen** bee's eggs. The eggs are in the egg cells.

Some insects are different. Ants, termites, wasps, and some bees live together in a **colony**. They take very good care of their eggs and young.

Hatching Eggs

When the eggs **hatch,** some types of insect young look very different than their parents. These are called **larvae.** Many larvae eat their old egg cases.

larva

egg case

These ladybug larvae do not look like their parents.

This dragonfly nymph hatches and lives under water.

Other types of insect young look more like their parents. These are called **nymphs**. The nymphs do not have wings. Some live under water.

Finding Food

Nymphs and **larvae** are always hungry!
Some eat large amounts of leaves and fruit.

The larvae of butterflies and moths are called caterpillars.

ant

ant lion larva

This ant lion larva digs a hole in the sand and waits to attack passing ants.

Other young insects attack and eat other animals. Many eat other insects.

Caring for the Young

Most insects do not take care of their young. They may even eat them! Insects that live in **colonies** do take care of their eggs and **larvae**.

larva

ant

These ants take care of their young in underground nests.

grub

Worker honeybees bring their **grubs** food to eat.

Insects in colonies often have a special room they keep their eggs and young in. They bring their young food to eat.

Staying Hidden

Many animals eat young insects. Some young insects try to stay hidden from their **enemies**. They are often the same color as the plants they live on.

These Kentish glory moth caterpillars stay hidden by being the same color as the leaves they eat.

Some **nymphs** that live in water need to hide from hungry fish. They make a home out of small pieces of plant and sand. They carry their homes around with them.

This caddis fly nymph is hard to spot.

Stay Away!

Some insects have a horrible taste.
Their bright colors warn **predators** that
they taste bad.

Cinnabar moth caterpillars taste horrible.

The black dots on this woolly slug caterpillar look like big scary eyes.

Another way insects keep from being eaten is to surprise their **enemies**. Some insects try to make themselves look like a bigger animal to scare their enemies.

Amazing Changes

As insect **larvae** grow they get too big for their skin. Their skin splits and they climb out, with bigger skin. This is called **shedding**.

old skin

This ladybug larva is shedding its skin.

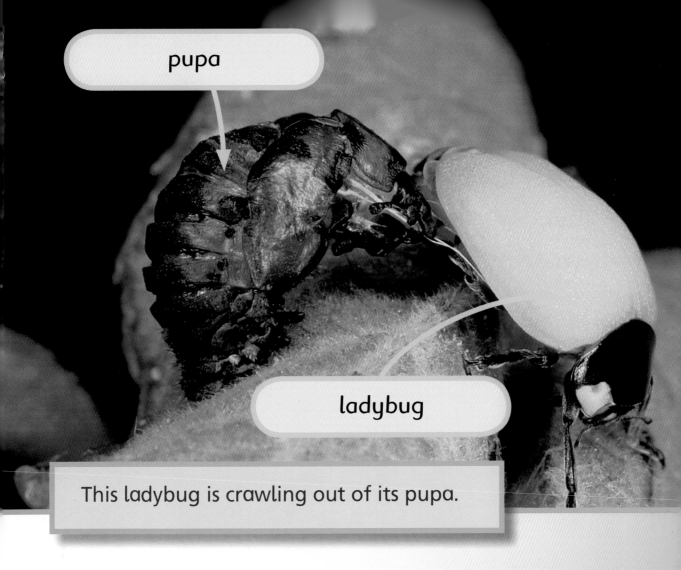

pupa

ladybug

This ladybug is crawling out of its pupa.

The skin sheds for the last time leaving a **pupa**. Inside the pupa the larva is changing. Soon it splits open and the adult insect comes out.

Splitting Skins

Nymphs do not turn into **pupae**. They already look a lot like an adult insect. When they are big enough they **shed** their skins for the very last time.

This dragonfly nymph has climbed out of the water and is ready to shed its skin.

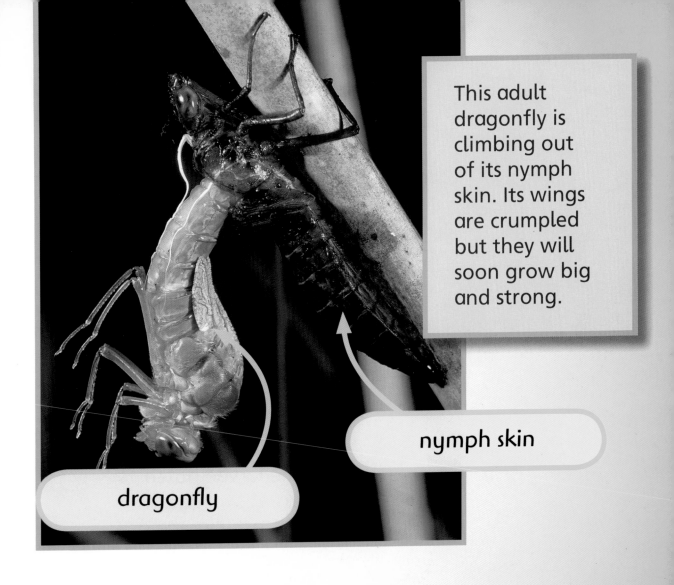

This adult dragonfly is climbing out of its nymph skin. Its wings are crumpled but they will soon grow big and strong.

nymph skin

dragonfly

The adult insect climbs out of the nymph skin. The new adult insect often stays very still while blood pumps around its new body.

Insect Life Cycles

This is how an insect **larva** grows up.
The larva does not look like its parents.

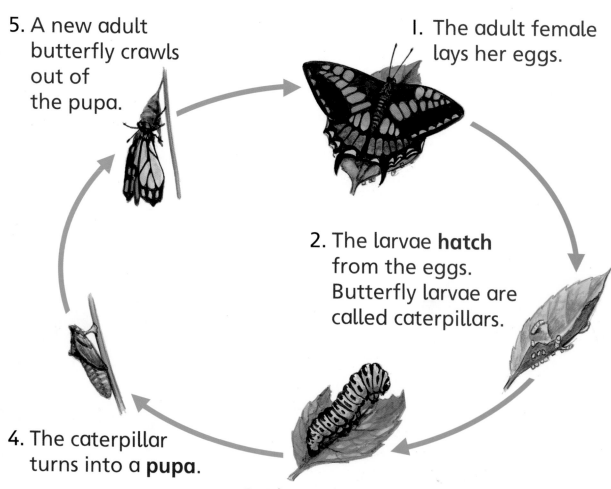

5. A new adult butterfly crawls out of the pupa.

1. The adult female lays her eggs.

2. The larvae **hatch** from the eggs. Butterfly larvae are called caterpillars.

4. The caterpillar turns into a **pupa**.

3. The caterpillars eat a lot of food. They grow bigger and bigger.

This is how an insect **nymph** grows up.
The nymph looks a lot like its parents.

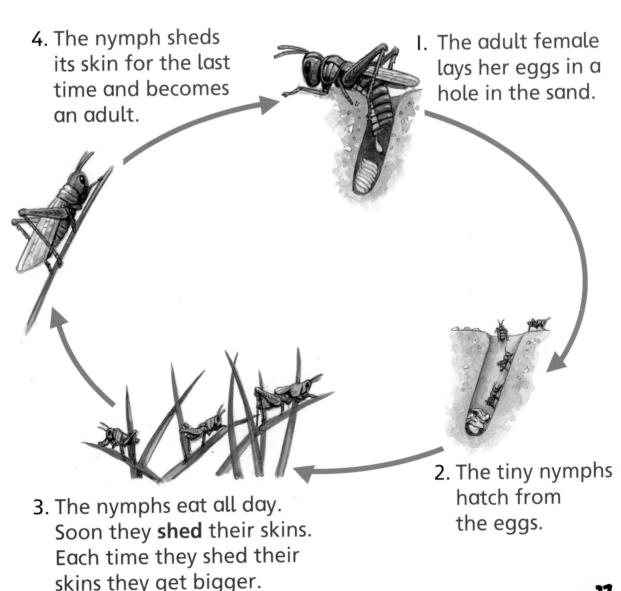

4. The nymph sheds its skin for the last time and becomes an adult.

1. The adult female lays her eggs in a hole in the sand.

3. The nymphs eat all day. Soon they **shed** their skins. Each time they shed their skins they get bigger.

2. The tiny nymphs hatch from the eggs.

Insects and Other Animals

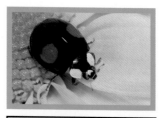

		INSECTS	
WHAT THEY LOOK LIKE:	Bones inside body	none	
	Number of legs	6	
	Hair on body	all	
	Scaly skin	none	
	Wings	most	
	Feathers	none	
WHERE THEY LIVE:	On land	most	
	In water	some	
HOW THEY ARE BORN:	Grows babies inside body	some	
	Lays eggs	most	
HOW THEY FEED YOUNG:	Feeds baby milk	none	
	Brings baby food	some	

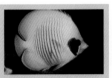

MAMMALS	FISH	AMPHIBIANS	BIRDS	REPTILES
all	all	all	all	all
none, 2, or 4	none	4 or none	2	4 or none
all	none	none	none	none
few	most	none	none	all
some	none	none	all	none
none	none	none	all	none
most	none	most	all	most
some	all	some	none	some
most	some	few	none	some
few	most	most	all	most
all	none	none	none	none
most	none	none	most	none

Incredible Insects!

- There are many more insects in the world than any other type of animal. Scientists have found more than I million species of insects, but they think there could be millions more.

- Some small creepy-crawlies may look a bit like insects, but if you look closely, you can see they are not. Spiders, worms, and snails are not insects. They do not have six legs.

- The longest insect in the world is a type of stick insect. It can grow as long as your arm.

Stick insect

Glossary

burrow hole that an animal makes in the ground to live or hide eggs in

colony group of insects that live together

enemy animal that will kill another animal for food or for its home

grub type of larva

hatch to be born from an egg

larva (more than one = larvae) animal baby that hatches from an egg but looks different than an adult

nymph young insect that looks like an adult insect when it is born

predator animal that hunts and kills other animals for food

pupa (more than one = pupae) shell of skin that a larva grows inside

queen mother insect

shed to lose an old layer of skin when a new, bigger one has grown

workers ants or bees that do all the work in a colony, such as feeding the young

Find out More

Books

Ganeri, Anita. *How Living Things Grow: From Caterpillar to Butterfly*. Chicago: Heinemann Library, 2006.

Spilsbury, Louise and Richard. *From Egg to Adult: The Life Cycle of Insects*. Heinemann Library, 2003.

Website

www.pestworldforkids.org

Index